modern patterns

CIRCULAR

coloring book

MindWare®
® brainy toys for kids of all ages®

www.mindware.com

MindWare Original Coloring Books

Dazzling patterns, optical illusions, hidden images and intricate details provide hours of imaginative fun. Our artist-quality art supplies are the perfect companions. Visit www.mindware.com to see our full selection.

40096
24 Fine Tip Markers

....

52150
18 Colored Pencils

56191 **Mystery Mosaics: Book 1**

25075 **Hidden Fur**

80185 **PrismDesigns**

40010 **Illuminations Optical Art**

36020 **Hidden Transformations**

48150 **Color Counts: Animals**

91007 **EnviroScapes**

36017 **Modern Patterns Illusions**

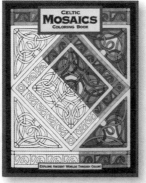

15003 **Celtic Mosaics**

95120 **EcoLights**

ISBN 978-1-933054-23-0
SKU 32000

MindWare.
brainy toys for kids of all ages®

for other MindWare products visit
www.mindware.com

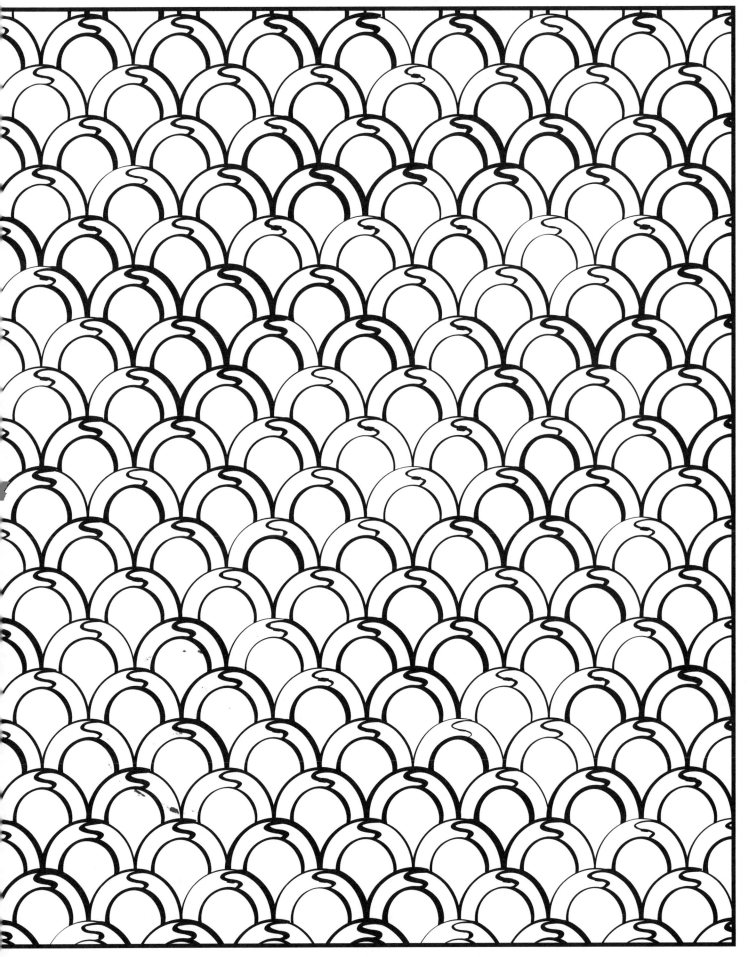

Modern Patterns **Circular**

Modern Patterns **Circular**

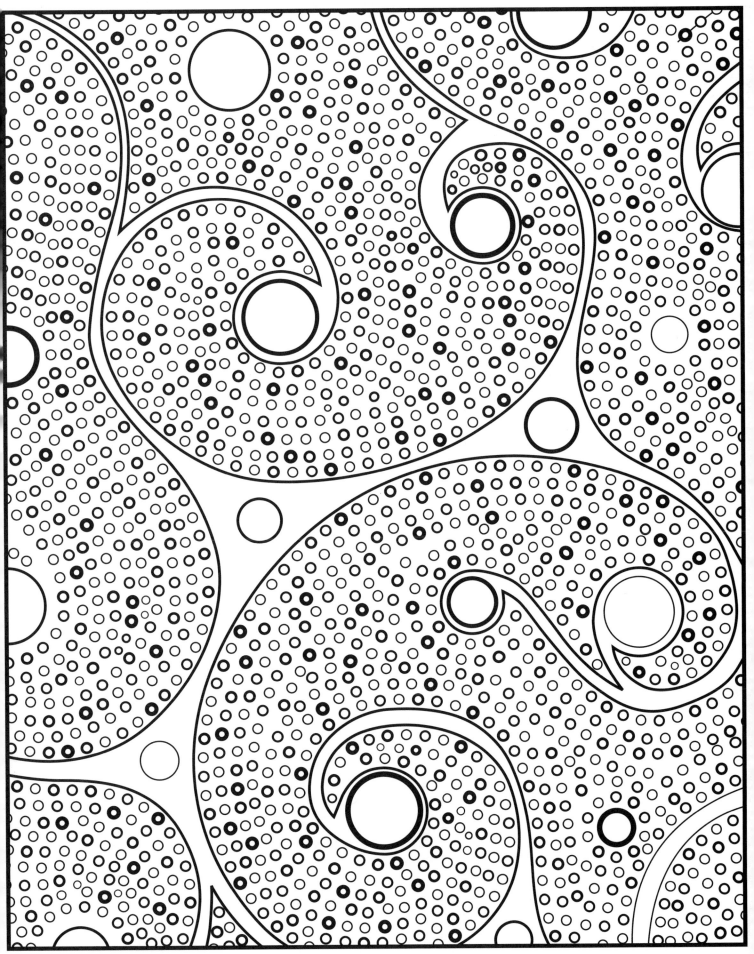

Modern Patterns **Circular**

Modern Patterns **Circular**

Modern Patterns **Circular**

Modern Patterns **Circular**

Modern Patterns **Circular**

Modern Patterns **Circular**